Contents

written by Pam Holden

1

Tides are the rise and fall of the sea. Changes in the tide happen along the coasts and in rivers near the sea. High tide is when the water is deeper and comes up high on the shore. Low tide is when the water is shallower and does not come up so far.

Tides change because the moon and the sun pull on the oceans and make them rise. The moon pulls more strongly than the sun because it is closer to Earth. High tides happen as the sea rises, and low tides happen as it falls. Most places have two high tides and two low tides every day.

Each month there are two special tides called spring tides. The name has nothing to do with the season spring, but is because the sea rises higher. Spring tides happen when the moon and the sun are in line with Earth and they pull together.

Spring tides have a big difference between high tides and low tides — high tides are extra high and low tides are very low.

5

There are also two tides each month called neap tides, which are the opposite to high tides. Neap tides happen when the moon and the sun are in two different directions and they do not pull together.

Neap tides do not rise and fall very much, so they have only a small difference between high tides and low tides.

7

Sometimes strong winds and storms make tides come up much higher than usual. Sea walls have been built to stop damage from huge waves.

Some rivers near coasts have special barriers to stop tidal waves from flowing up the rivers into cities and towns.

Tides are important to people for work and play. Tide times are about an hour later each day, so there are charts to tell when high and low tides will happen. Fishermen need to know the best times to move their boats and to catch fish.

Big ships need to move in and out of ports and bays at high tide, when the water is deeper. For swimmers, it is safer when the water is flowing in than when the tide is pulling out. Surfers get a better ride as big waves push them in to shore.

Along rocky coasts there are reefs and tide pools that are home to many sea animals and plants. Fish swim in with the tide to feed on seaweed, shellfish, and small fish. Fishermen know that high tide is a good time to catch fish there.

Shellfish open their shells to feed at high tide. But when the tide is low, they close their shells and dig into the sand to hide. Hungry seabirds hunt along the shore for plants and animals.

At low tide, people can explore the rocky tide pools. They see beautiful anemones living there, with starfish moving slowly on the sand. Limpets and periwinkles stick tightly to the rocks, so they won't be washed away by strong tides. Crabs and octopuses move in and out of cracks in the rocks, while snails and hermit crabs hide inside their shells.

Shellfish are delicious food, so some people like
to go to the shore at low tide to dig for them in
the sand. Other people, called beachcombers,
find pretty shells, pieces of driftwood, and
treasures that have come in with the tide.

High tides bring clean water from the deep sea to ports, beaches, and bays. This helps to keep them healthy and fresh for the sea animals that live there, and for people to enjoy.